curiousabout
ROBOTS
IN FICTION

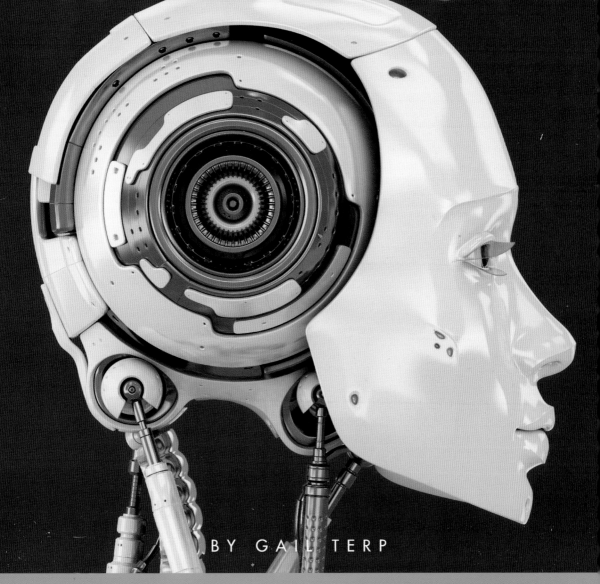

T0276659

BY GAIL TERP

AMICUS LEARNING

What are you

curious about?

CHAPTER THREE
3

Robots and Science
PAGE
16

Curious about is published by
Amicus Learning, an imprint of Amicus
P.O. Box 227
Mankato, MN 56002
www.amicuspublishing.us

Editor: Rebecca Glaser
Series and Book Designer: Kathleen Petelinsek
Photo researcher: Omay Ayres

Library of Congress Cataloging-in-Publication Data
Names: Terp, Gail, 1951– author.
Title: Curious about robots in fiction / by Gail Terp.
Description: Mankato, MN : Amicus Learning, an imprint of
Amicus, [2024] | Series: Curious about robotics | Includes
bibliographical references and index. | Audience: Ages 5–9 |
Audience: Grades 2–3 | Summary: "Questions and answers give
kids an understanding about the technology of robots in fiction,
including why there are so many robots in fiction and if they
hold up to actual science. Includes infographics to support visual
learning and back matter to support research skills, plus a glossary
and index"—Provided by publisher.
Identifiers: LCCN 2023013266 (print) | LCCN 2023013267
(ebook) | ISBN 9781645496557 (library binding) | ISBN
9781681529448 (paperback) | ISBN 9781645496816 (pdf)
Subjects: LCSH: Robots in popular culture–Juvenile literature. |
Robots in motion pictures–Juvenile literature. | Robots on television–
Juvenile literature. | Robots in literature–Juvenile literature.
Classification: LCC TJ211.2 .T37 2024 (print) | LCC TJ211.2
(ebook) | DDC 629.8/92–dc23/eng/20230330
LC record available at https://lccn.loc.gov/2023013266
LC ebook record available at https://lccn.loc.gov/2023013267

Photo credits: Alamy/Entertainment Pictures, 9, PictureLux / The
Hollywood Archive, 10–11, 13; Dreamstime/Vladislav Ociacia,
cover; MIT/CSAIL/Massachusetts Institute of Technology, 3,
19, 20, 21; Shutterstock/Little Adventures, 7; Shutterstock/
metamorworks, 23, Warut Chinsai, 2, 14; Wikimedia
Commons/Heinz Schulz-Neudamm/MoMA, 5, IMP Awards,
2, 6, 8, John R. Neill, 5, Karel Capek, 5, William Tung, 13

Printed in China

CHAPTER ONE

Are robots in fiction a new thing?

Not at all! L. Frank Baum wrote *Ozma of Oz* back in 1907. It featured Tik Tok, one of the first fictional robots. The first robot movie was *Metropolis*. It came out in 1927.

From books to plays to movies, writers love to feature robot characters.

DID YOU KNOW?

The play *R.U.R.* came out in 1920. It was the first time the word *robot* was used.

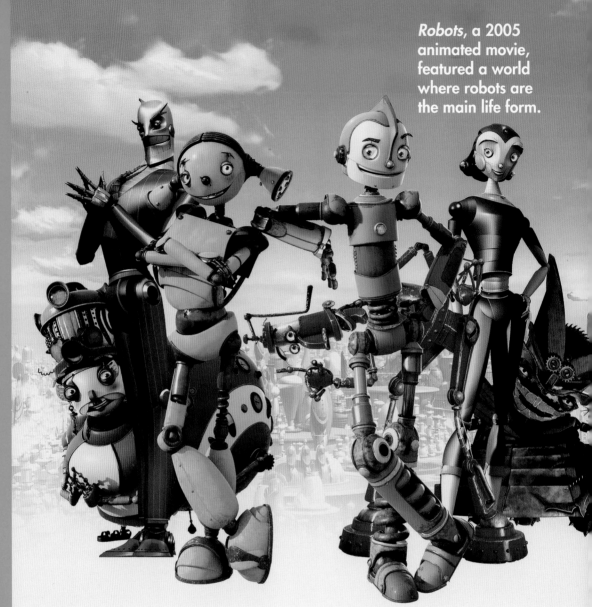

Robots, a 2005 animated movie, featured a world where robots are the main life form.

Why do people like to write about robots?

In movies for adults, robots can be evil and scary.

Well, most robots are fun! Of course, not all are fun. Some can be downright evil. Robots are a perfect tool for writers and filmmakers. They help tell the story. And some even teach lessons.

What kind of lessons could a robot teach?

In *Ron's Gone Wrong*, Barney discovers that a B-bot is no substitute for a real friend.

All kinds! The *Iron Giant* teaches that we can **overcome** bad things. *WALL-E* tells us that we need to take better care of our environment. The robot in *Ron's Gone Wrong* shows that real-life friendships are important.

In the movie, Wall-E is the last working robot cleaning up a destroyed Earth. Then he discovers a single plant.

WALL-E
FUN FACTS
Name means:
Waste **A**llocation **L**oad **L**ifter: **E**arth class
Eyes inspired by real binoculars.
Top speed 35 mph (56 km/h)

CHAPTER TWO

What is the most famous fictional robot?

C-3PO and R2-D2 help Rebel forces in *Star Wars.*

Hard to say! However, *Star Wars* has two of the most famous movie robots. R2-D2 is a **mechanic** robot. He **communicates** in beeps and whistles. C-3PO is more human-like. He talks and worries a lot. He's also very loyal.

HEIGHT COMPARISON
C-3PO 5 feet 9 inches (1.75 m)
R2-D2 3 feet 7 inches (1.09 m)

Are there also robots on television?

Yes! The first two came out in the 1960s. *Lost in Space* was set in 1997. It featured a family stuck on a faraway planet. Their Robot B-9 was super strong and fun. *The Jetsons* featured a family living in 2062. They had a robot maid, Rosie.

DID YOU KNOW?
Voltron: Legendary Defender is an animated robot series on Netflix.

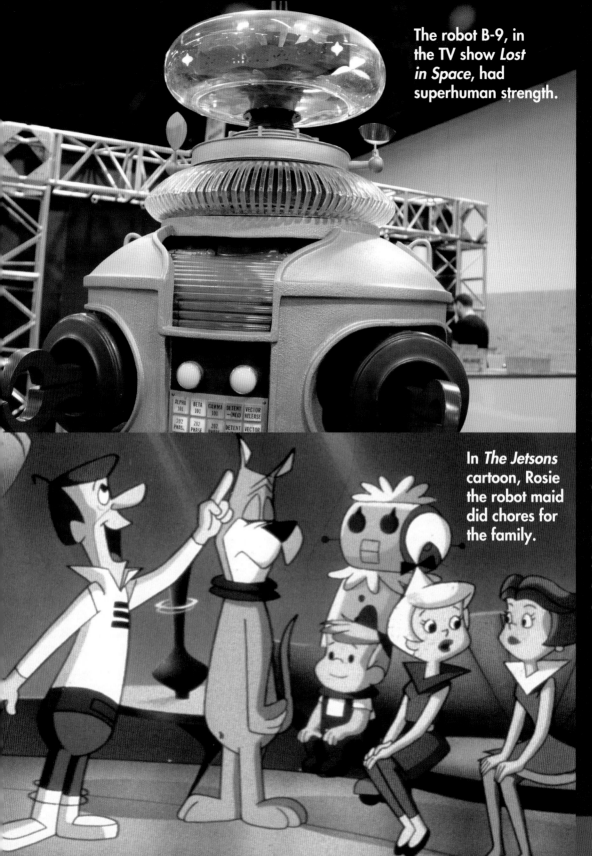

The robot B-9, in the TV show *Lost in Space*, had superhuman strength.

In *The Jetsons* cartoon, Rosie the robot maid did chores for the family.

Have any TV robots been in movies?

Transformers began as a cartoon TV series in 1984. In it, two groups of **alien** robots are at war. In 2007, the first of many Transformer movies came out. And new Transformer movies are still being made.

DID YOU KNOW?
Transformer **merchandise** makes more money than the movies.

A robot made from scrap metal and car parts was inspired by the Transformers.

CHAPTER THREE

Are movie robots based on real science?

The origami robot from MIT can open itself from a flat sheet in less than four minutes!

For sure, some movie robots are based on science. For example, consider the Transformers. They are robots that can change themselves into other things. At first, this was just fiction. Today, **origami** robots are a real thing. They can change themselves from a flat sheet to a structure. It only takes minutes!

Do scientists watch robot movies?

Some do. Maja Matarić is a robot expert. She creates robots that help others. When she was a student, she was a fan of the Star Wars movies. She and her student friends all watched them. Matarić is still a fan and has a bunch of little R2-D2s in her office.

IS Robotics

Science fiction can inspire scientists like Maja Matarić to create new inventions.

Self-driving cars
are not common yet.
They cost much more
than other cars.

Are there real inventions based on fictional robots?

Driving

Absolutely! "Sally" came out in 1953. It was a story about self-driving cars. Self-driving cars now exist. Soon they may be everywhere. The Jetson family had a vacuum robot. These days, lots of homes have them. Some even wash floors.

ASK MORE QUESTIONS

How tall do movie robots get?

Was there an actor inside C-3PO?

Try a BIG QUESTION: I want to make a robot movie. Where would I learn how to do it?

SEARCH FOR ANSWERS

Search the library catalog or the Internet.
A librarian, teacher, or parent can help you.

Using Keywords
Find the looking glass.

Keywords are the most important words in your question.

?

If you want to know about:

- tall movie robots, type: TALLEST MOVIE ROBOTS

- C-3PO, type: C-3PO ACTOR

FIND GOOD SOURCES

Are the sources reliable?

Some sources are better than others. An adult can help you. Here are some good, safe sources.

Books

Robots from Then to Now
by Rachel Grack, 2020.

The Robot Book
by Rebecca Silverstein, 2020.

Internet Sites

How Big Is the World's Largest Robot?
*https://www.wonderopolis.org/wonder/
how-big-is-the-worlds-largest-robot*
Read all about a truly huge robot.

How to Make a Robot
*https://www.futurelearn.com/info/
blog/how-to-make-a-robot*
First read some interesting robot information.
Then learn how to make your own robot.

Every effort has been made to ensure that these
websites are appropriate for children. However,
because of the nature of the Internet, it is impossible
to guarantee that these sites will remain active
indefinitely or that their contents will not be altered.

SHARE AND TAKE ACTION

Research

With an adult, research how to make your own robot. You can start with the link found at left.

Thinking about robots of the future?

Borrow robot movies from the library. Then think up new robots!

Be creative!

Write a story about a robot that saves your town!

GLOSSARY

alien From a place that is not Earth.

communicate To share thoughts, ideas, or information so they are understood.

mechanic A robot or person that fixes machines.

merchandise Goods that are bought and sold.

origami The Japanese art of folding paper into shapes.

overcome To defeat a problem or enemy.

INDEX

About the Author

After teaching for years, Gail Terp now has a second dream job: writing books for kids. Her books are about all sorts of topics. Now she has a new topic. Robots! When not writing, she loves walking around looking for interesting stuff to write about.